EVERGREEN CHRIS

AND THE

MAGIC SEED

A "Save our Space" recycle series

Written and Illustrated By

Mary Casey-Griffin

To order additional copies of this book, contact:
Xlibris
1-888-795-4274
www.Xlibris.com
Orders@Xlibris.com

ISBN: Softcover   978-1-7960-6457-5
          EBook   978-1-7960-6456-8

Print information available on the last page

Rev. date: 10/09/2019

This Book is dedicated
to
Stan and Michael Griffin
Two of my favorite readers!

In the middle of the forest, the wind blew one fall day and a seed from an evergreen tree sank into the earth.

The winter made the ground hard with frost and snow. Tucked in, the little seed lay sleeping until warmer weather.

When the spring came and the ground got soft, the little seed woke and pushed his way up through the dirt. At first, he was very skinny with small branches that could bend very easily.

Each day, when the sun rose high in the sky, he could feel the warmth on its branches. This made them grow faster. His trunk also grew thicker, making him stand very straight.

Soon, he felt little tickles on his branches. He looked around and saw that birds of many different colors were resting and playing on them.

The little tree was becoming happier and happier, knowing that he was very useful.

Then, he felt the scurry of little feet up and down his trunk. The squirrels had found a home where they could build their nests.

The little tree was having such a good time, growing and growing, while making friends with all the little animals. The years went by and he grew to be quite tall. The other trees named him Chris because he looked like the perfect Christmas tree.

Then, one winter, there was a happy buzz in the air. "Which one of us will be picked to decorate the house of a special family?", they asked each other.

And then it happened! A family came to look for a Christmas tree. They were all so excited to pick one out! The trees stretched out their arms as straight as they could to impress the child.

After Chris was placed on top of the car, the family traveled to their home. Then they placed him in a pot of water in the corner of the living room.

And then they put colorful lights and decorations on his branches and flipped the switch. Oh, he looked so beautiful!

Chris happily stood in the living room for about a month. Then it was time to take him down from his special stand.

They placed him on their car and took Chris to the local recycling center. This is a place where you can take things that you can't use anymore, like branches, mulch and even glass bottles.

The man at the recycling center smiles as he tells the dad to drop Chris off in the corner by the big machine.

Everyone said goodbye to their bushy, green friend.
Then the man turned on the big machine.

The machine comes to life and gently grabs Chris and pushes him through it. He comes out in little pieces called mulch.

When it is finished, the man puts the mulch into a big storage bin. The mulch will stay there until spring, when the ground warms up again.

People came to take
this mulch

To their Gardens

They spread it
all around

Their flowers
and trees!

Printed in the United States
By Bookmasters